SEX COUPONS

To: ❤ — — — — — — — — — — — ❤

50 Promises Just For You

THIS COUPON IS GOOD FOR:

Have a whipped cream night! (You place it I'll lick it)

THIS COUPON IS GOOD FOR:

Slow sensual foreplay

THIS COUPON IS GOOD FOR:

A full body massage with oil (orgasm included)

THIS COUPON IS GOOD FOR:

Servant for a day/ A"Yes Day"

THIS COUPON IS GOOD FOR:

New sexy lingerie

THIS COUPON IS GOOD FOR:

Oral pleasure

THIS COUPON IS GOOD FOR:

Bubble bath for two with wine

THIS COUPON IS GOOD FOR:

Sunday Funday!
(afternoon sex
every Sunday for
a month!)

THIS COUPON IS GOOD FOR:

Car fun

THIS COUPON IS GOOD FOR:

6 9

THIS COUPON IS GOOD FOR:

Bondage sex/ tied hands

THIS COUPON IS GOOD FOR:

A new sex toy

THIS COUPON IS GOOD FOR:

Sexy striptease

THIS COUPON IS GOOD FOR:

Get fingered
in a public place

THIS COUPON IS GOOD FOR:

Strip poker game

THIS COUPON IS GOOD FOR:

Shower fun

THIS COUPON IS GOOD FOR:

Erotic

Movie Night

THIS COUPON IS GOOD FOR:

Sweet fun:

sex & chocolate

THIS COUPON IS GOOD FOR:

Morning sex

THIS COUPON IS GOOD FOR:

Skinny-Dipping

THIS COUPON IS GOOD FOR:

Romantic dinner

&

breakfast in bed

THIS COUPON IS GOOD FOR:

Quickie
in a public place

THIS COUPON IS GOOD FOR:

Private

photo shoot

THIS COUPON IS GOOD FOR:

Hotel room

THIS COUPON IS GOOD FOR:

A sexual fantasy you have

THIS COUPON IS GOOD FOR:

Role playing

teacher-student,

nurse-patient, ...

THIS COUPON IS GOOD FOR:

Longest
kiss ever

THIS COUPON IS GOOD FOR:

2 new

sex positions

THIS COUPON IS GOOD FOR:

Private

Sex Tape

THIS COUPON IS GOOD FOR:

50 kisses, not on the lips

THIS COUPON IS GOOD FOR:

THIS COUPON IS GOOD FOR:

THIS COUPON IS GOOD FOR:

THIS COUPON IS GOOD FOR:

THIS COUPON IS GOOD FOR:

THIS COUPON IS GOOD FOR:

THIS COUPON IS GOOD FOR:

THIS COUPON IS GOOD FOR:

THIS COUPON IS GOOD FOR:

THIS COUPON IS GOOD FOR:

THIS COUPON IS GOOD FOR:

THIS COUPON IS GOOD FOR:

THIS COUPON IS GOOD FOR:

THIS COUPON IS GOOD FOR:

THIS COUPON IS GOOD FOR:

THIS COUPON IS GOOD FOR:

THIS COUPON IS GOOD FOR:

THIS COUPON IS GOOD FOR:

Printed in Great Britain
by Amazon

14184235R00059